Symbols of
American Freedom

The Alamo

by Michael Burgan

Series Consultant: Jerry D. Thompson,
Regents Professor of History,
Texas A&M International University

CHELSEA CLUBHOUSE
An Imprint of Chelsea House Publishers

Symbols of American Freedom: The Alamo

Chelsea Clubhouse
An imprint of Chelsea House Publishers
132 West 31st Street
New York NY 10001

Library of Congress Cataloging-in-Publication Data
Burgan, Michael.
        The Alamo / by Michael Burgan.
            p. cm. — (Symbols of American freedom)
        Includes index.
        ISBN 978-1-60413-512-1
    1. Alamo (San Antonio, Tex.)—Juvenile literature. 2. Alamo (San Antonio, Tex.)—Siege, 1836—Juvenile literature. 3. Texas—History—To 1846--Juvenile literature. 4. San Antonio (Tex.)—Buildings, structures, etc.—Juvenile literature. I. Title. II. Series.
    F390.B9124 2010
    976.4'03—dc22   2009002821

Developed for Chelsea House by RJF Publishing LLC (www.RJFpublishing.com)
Text and cover design by Tammy West/Westgraphix LLC
Maps by Stefan Chabluk
Photo research by Edward A. Thomas
Index by Nila Glikin

Photo Credits: cover, 41, 43: Shutterstock; 4, 5, 21, 32: iStockphoto; 6: Buena Vista/Photofest; 8, 11, 27: The Granger Collection, New York; 9, 25, 39: Alamy; 12: Austin's Colony, Settlement of, Courtesy State Preservation Board, Austin, TX, Photographer: Perry Huston, 1/5/95 Post Conservation; 16: Gonzales Flag, Courtesy State Preservation Board, Austin, TX, Accession ID: 809-002612, Photographer: Victor Hotho 8/31/2007, Post Conservation; 33: Surrender of Santa Anna 1989.46, Courtesy State Preservation Board, Austin, TX, Original Artist: Huddle, William H., 1847 – 1892, Photographer: unknown, Pre 1991, Pre Conservation / (c) State Preservation Board (2009), Austin, Texas. All rights reserved, including further reproduction, commercial display, incorporation into other works, or conversion to digital media; 13, 15: North Wind Picture Archives; 24: Library of Congress LC-USZ62-93521; 30: Friends of the Governor's Mansion, Austin, TX; 31: Library of Congress LC-USZ62-110029; 37: U.S. Air Force photo/Steve Thurow.

Table of Contents

Words that are defined in the Glossary are in **bold** type the
first time they appear in the text.

"Remember the Alamo"

Chapter 1

On March 6, 1836, almost 2,000 Mexican troops prepared for battle. Their target was a Texas fort called the Alamo. Inside, fewer than 200 men waited to defend the fort. They knew they could not beat the Mexicans. But they were ready to die rather than give up.

The defenders of the Alamo were fighting for Texas's freedom. At the time, Texas was part of Mexico. But just a few days before, Texians (as people of Texas were called then) had declared their independence from Mexico. Mexican General Antonio López de Santa Anna thought that the Texians were **rebels**. Santa Anna was the leader of Mexico at the time, and he commanded the Mexican troops outside the Alamo.

Around 5 A.M. on March 6, the Mexican soldiers stormed the fort. The defenders inside fired cannons and rifles. They killed or wounded hundreds of Mexicans. But the attackers entered the fort. Within two hours, the Mexicans had taken the Alamo. The Texians were defeated.

Parts of the Alamo still stand today in the city of San Antonio, Texas. This building at the Alamo was first used as a small church (or chapel).

In this scene from the movie *The Alamo*, actors play Alamo heroes William Travis, Davy Crockett, and James Bowie.

The war for Texas independence was not over. Santa Anna sent his troops farther into Texas. They won several small battles. They also killed hundreds of prisoners held at a fort in Goliad. Then, in April, Santa Anna fought the Texians at San Jacinto.

By this time, the Texian soldiers were led by Sam Houston. They were able to surprise Santa Anna and his army. As the Texians charged, the men shouted, "Remember the Alamo! Remember Goliad!" Thinking of the courage of the Alamo defenders helped the Texians fight bravely at the battle of San Jacinto. They defeated Santa Anna's army. With this victory, the Texians won their independence from Mexico.

People and Names in Texas

Today, the people of Texas are called Texans. But in the 1830s, different names were used for different people there. A Texian was an **Anglo**, a white person not of Spanish or Mexican descent, who had come to Texas from the United States. An **immigrant** from Europe was also called a Texian. A Tejano was a Texas resident who came from a Spanish-speaking family (a woman would be called a Tejana). In this book, Texians is often used to refer to all the people in Texas seeking independence. This includes Tejanos and African Americans.

Early Years of the Alamo

Today the Alamo is remembered as a famous fort. But it first had another use. In the early 1700s, when Spain ruled Texas, the Alamo was built as a **mission**—a church with other buildings and land around it. Roman Catholic priests lived at the mission and tried to teach Christianity to the local Indians. The Alamo was then called the mission of San Antonio de Valero. The town that grew up around the mission was later called San Antonio.

At the mission, Native Americans who became Christians worked and lived with the priests. The Indians raised crops and animals for the Spanish. By 1793, most of the Indians at the mission had died from disease. The Spanish government closed the mission. In 1803, Spanish troops arrived to use it as a fort. They came from a part of Mexico called Alamo de Parras. Soon, the former mission was known as the Alamo. Historians are not certain if the fort's name came from the name of this town. The name might also refer to the Spanish word for the cottonwood tree—*alamo*. These trees are very common around San Antonio.

The Alamo's Defenders

The story of the Alamo and the Texas Revolution soon became part of U.S. history. In 1845, Texas became the 28th U.S. state. Even before then, Americans knew about the bravery of the Alamo defenders. Most of those defenders had lived in the United States before moving to Texas and becoming Texians. These men included William Travis and James Bowie. Other defenders of the Alamo had gone to Texas in 1835 and 1836 just to help the Texians win their freedom. The most famous of these fighters was Davy Crockett. The defenders also included men with Mexican roots. One of them was Juan Seguín. He was not at the Alamo on March 6, but before the battle he had helped prepare for the coming attack. Seguín later fought the Mexicans at San Jacinto. At least one African American also fought and died at the Alamo.

The fierce fighting between Mexican troops and the Texian defenders of the Alamo is shown in this picture from the 1800s.

Learning and Remembering

The fight to defend the Alamo still interests many people. Some Americans use the cry "Remember the Alamo!" to recall great bravery during times of trouble. That memory stirs their own courage. Even people from other countries have admired the Alamo defenders. The battle reminds them of heroes in their own nation's past.

Today, parts of the Alamo are still standing. The site is called a **shrine**. Visitors come to honor the brave defenders. They also learn about the history of the fort and the fight for Texas independence. The Alamo helps people remember the price some people have paid to win or keep their freedom.

Changing Views on the Alamo

Historians use many tools to learn what happened in the past. Letters, government records, and newspapers all help. So does studying items found at historic sites. Historians are still learning new facts about the Alamo and its defenders. Over time, historians also change their minds about parts of the story of an important place or event. For many years, U.S. historians focused on the Anglos at the Alamo. Many did not closely study the Tejanos there. Now, people know more about their important role. Historians also debate some issues because the records do not agree. No one knows exactly how many people defended the Alamo or how many Mexicans were killed during the battle.

Every year Texans celebrate Independence Day on March 2, the day in 1836 when Texas declared its independence from Mexico. A parade (above) is held in Austin, the state capital.

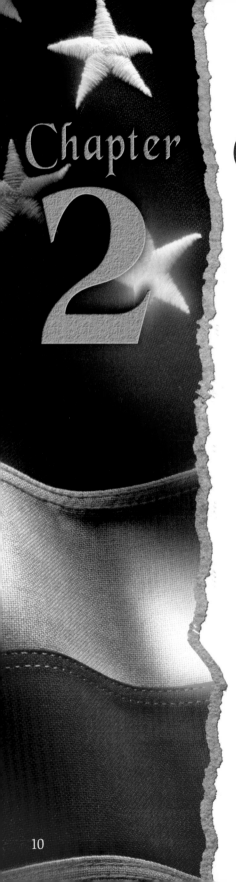

Americans Come to Texas

L ed by Hernán Cortés, the first Spanish soldiers arrived in Mexico in 1519. Over the next two years, they defeated the Aztecs and other Indians who lived there and took control of their lands. Mexico became a Spanish **colony**. The Spanish soon expanded their control in all directions. By 1810, Mexico included a great deal of land that is now part of the United States, including Texas.

That year, Mexicans began a revolution against Spain. They wanted their independence. The revolution lasted for more than ten years, until Mexico gained its independence in 1821. Before and during this revolution, a few Americans moved to Texas from the United States. In 1820, Moses Austin hoped to bring even more there.

Spain had once tried to keep Americans and other foreigners out of Texas. It wanted total control over all its lands. But Spanish leaders changed their policy and decided to let Austin come to Texas. They

Before the Americans

The Spanish first reached Texas in the 1500s. Different Indian tribes lived there at the time. These included the Karankawas and Caddos. The Comanches, Apaches, and other tribes came later. Spanish settlers and Indians sometimes married. The children of these marriages were called *mestizos*. This Spanish word means "mixed." Mestizos in Texas had more legal rights than slaves and Indians. But the mestizos had fewer rights than the Spanish. People born in Spain or who had two Spanish parents held most of the power across Mexico and Texas.

After getting horses from the Spanish, the Comanches became skilled riders.

gave him land near the Brazos and Colorado Rivers. (The Colorado River in Texas is a different river from the Colorado River that flows through the Grand Canyon and several states in the southwestern United States.) Austin was happy when he heard the news, but he never did get to bring settlers to Texas. He died a few months later in June 1821. Before his death, Austin said his son Stephen should take the settlers into Texas.

Austin's Settlers

Stephen F. Austin had served in the military and worked in his father's business. He had also been in politics. His skills became useful as he tried to build his colony in Texas. By now, Mexico had won its independence. Its leaders agreed to the deal Spain had made with Austin's father. Stephen Austin made plans for 300 American families to settle in Texas.

Stephen F. Austin (center) talks with settlers at his new colony in Texas.

They would receive land to farm. Austin also started a small town called San Felipe de Austin. It became the capital of his settlement.

In 1824, Mexico changed its government. It now had elected leaders and a **constitution**, just as the United States did. Austin supported these changes. The Mexican government also linked Texas to a region called Coahuila. Together they formed the Mexican state of Coahuila y Texas. Over the next few years, more Americans came to Austin's colony in

Slavery in Texas

By law, Spain did not allow slavery in Texas. But in 1821, Spanish officials agreed to let Austin and his settlers bring slaves with them to their new lands. Some Tejanos in Texas also owned slaves. By 1825, more than 400 of the people on Austin's lands were slaves. Slavery was also illegal under Mexican law. Texians avoided this law by saying their slaves were servants. They made the slaves sign contracts that forced them to work for their masters for 99 years. When Texas won its independence, it made slavery legal. Slavery continued to be legal in Texas until the Civil War (1861–1865). After the Civil War, slavery became illegal everywhere in the United States.

Antonio López de Santa Anna (1794–1876)

Antonio López de Santa Anna was born in Mexico in 1794. He joined the army while still in his teens. Santa Anna first fought for the forces that wanted Mexico to remain part of Spain. Later he supported independence and making Mexico a **republic**. From the 1830s to the 1850s, he served as president of Mexico several different times. As a general, Santa Anna was good at raising armies. But he lost several key battles, such as the one at San Jacinto. During the Mexican-American War (1846–1848), he led Mexican troops against U.S. forces that had invaded Mexico, and he was defeated in several battles. Santa Anna was often unpopular in Mexico. After he became president for the last time in the 1850s, he was overthrown and sent into **exile** for a number of years. He died in Mexico City in 1876.

Texas. They also settled in other areas nearby. The residents of Coahuila y Texas were far from Mexico's capital of Mexico City. They had a good deal of freedom to do what they liked. They worked hard and grew crops to sell at markets. Texas was now filling with Americans seeking land.

Troubles with Mexico

Some Mexican officials thought their government should take a more active role in Texas. They did not want the area to lose its ties to Mexico and perhaps become part of the United States. In 1830, the Mexican government passed a law intended to stop new settlers from the United States from entering Texas. It also ordered Mexican troops to be sent there. And the law said Texians could not bring more slaves to Texas. Many American settlers had brought slaves with them to work on their farms.

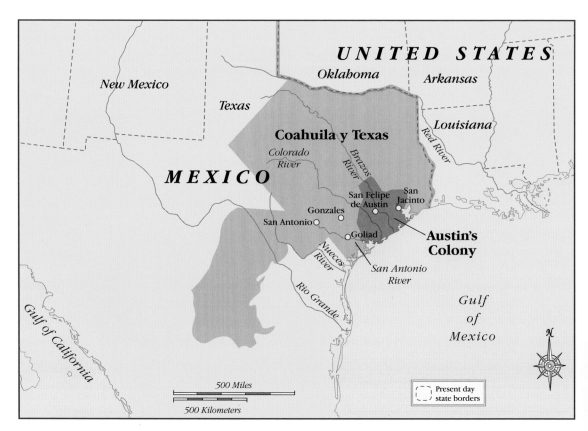

This map shows Texas in 1835, when it was part of the Mexican state of Coahuila y Texas. Only the eastern part of present-day Texas had been settled by Stephen F. Austin and other settlers from the United States.

The new law upset many Texians. They expected Texas to be settled by Americans. They also grew angry when Mexico tried to collect a tax on goods brought into Texas. Some of the money was used to build new forts in Texas. One of the forts was led by Colonel Juan David Bradburn. Some of the local Texians disliked him. In 1832, Bradburn arrested William Travis and sparked a small **rebellion**. The rebels forced Bradburn to release Travis, and Mexico removed Bradburn from the fort.

After this, more Texians thought Mexico was trying to limit their freedom. Some talked about declaring independence. Stephen Austin had another idea. He and other leading Texians wanted to split Texas from Coahuila. Mexico, however, rejected this. Austin wrote some letters saying the Texians should still plan to be a separate state some day. Mexican officials found these letters. They arrested Austin for **treason** in 1834 and sent him to jail.

General Santa Anna took control of Mexico's government in 1834 and began to rule as a **dictator**. When a rebellion broke out in the Mexican state of Zacatecas, the general led troops there and killed about 4,000 people. The dead included women and children.

Santa Anna next sent troops into Coahuila. They were led by his brother-in-law, General Martin Perfecto de Cos. In June 1835, Cos and his men shut down the state government and arrested local lawmakers.

In Their Own Words

Ready for War

Here is part of a statement Stephen Austin wrote in September 1835, after he started to believe that the Texians would have to fight against Mexico:

"...all kinds of [peaceful] measures with General Cos...are hopeless, and...nothing but ruin to Texas can be expected from any such measures.... War is our only resource. There is no other remedy but to defend our rights, our country, and ourselves by force of arms. To do this we must be united: and in order to unite the **delegates** of the people must meet...and organize a system of defense and give organization to the country so as to produce [joint action]."

This is the famous "Come and Take It" flag flown by the Texians at their fight with Mexican troops at Gonzales.

Some of the men who avoided arrest fled to Texas. One of them was James Bowie. He, Travis, and Sam Houston were among the Texians who wanted independence.

The Mexicans were again trying to collect taxes on Texian goods. The Texians also learned that Cos was heading to Texas. He planned to arrest officials there, as he had done in Coahuila. One person he wanted to arrest was Travis, who had helped free a Texian who had been arrested over taxes.

Stephen Austin was finally released from jail in August 1835. He still hoped to settle problems with Mexico peacefully. But the threat of war was growing. When Austin reached Texas, he saw that people were divided. Some agreed with him that the Texians should avoid war. Others were preparing to fight as Cos got closer to Texas.

In September, Cos's men boarded ships and sailed for the Texas coast. When the Mexicans landed, they headed for the fort at San Antonio. Now Austin changed his mind. He was ready to fight to defend Texas. So were many more Texians.

The First Shots

The Mexicans knew the Texians were preparing for war. In late September, about 100 Mexican troops went from San Antonio to the town of Gonzales. The Texians there had a small cannon, and the Mexicans wanted it. A group of armed citizens of Gonzales met the Mexicans when they reached the town. The citizens told the Mexican soldiers to "come and take it"—meaning the cannon.

The Mexicans pulled back and set up a camp. More Texians came into Gonzales, ready to fight. On October 2, they advanced on the Mexican camp. They brought the cannon with them. By now, they also had a flag showing the cannon (and also a star). Written on the flag were the words "Come and Take It." (This flag still exists and is now held by the Texas State Preservation Board.)

The Mexican commander did not want to fight. He met with a Texian to discuss the cannon. The Texians still refused to turn it over. They fired a few shots from the cannon and from their guns. The Mexicans fled after several of them were killed.

The Texians later called this small battle in Gonzales their Battle of Lexington. Lexington is the town just outside Boston, Massachusetts, that had been the site of the first battle of the American Revolution in April 1775. Now, sixty years later, in October 1835, the Texas Revolution had begun.

Siege in San Antonio

After the fighting at Gonzales, more Texians volunteered to fight the Mexicans. They marched to Goliad and took control of a fort there. The Mexican soldiers left the fort and went to San Antonio. General Cos had reached the city and was making the fort at the Alamo stronger. The Texians at Goliad took guns and supplies the Mexicans left behind.

More soldiers joined the growing Texian army. The men chose Stephen Austin as their general. James Bowie was made a colonel. Soon, Tejano volunteers led by Juan Seguín joined the force. In the town of Nacogdoches, residents picked Sam Houston to lead troops there. Houston wrote letters asking people in the United States to come to Texas and help fight the Mexicans.

Moving on San Antonio

On October 13, 1835, Austin began marching his troops to San Antonio. Fighting near the town began about two weeks later. Bowie led about 90 **cavalry** (soldiers on horseback) toward San Antonio. They met a force of about 400 Mexicans near a mission called Concepción. At first, fog made it hard to see. When the fog lifted, the Texians saw that they were surrounded. But some trees helped protect them from Mexican cannon fire. When the enemy tried to advance, Bowie's men shot many of them. The Mexicans finally retreated. They suffered about 60 **casualties** at this battle. Only one Texian had been killed, and only a few others had been wounded.

In November 1835, a total of 13 Texian towns sent delegates to an important meeting. The delegates would decide if Texas should declare its independence. At first, they said no. Texas would remain part of Mexico. But the fighting went on.

The Texians still wanted to defend their rights under the Mexican constitution. The delegates made Sam Houston the leader of the army since Austin was ill. Austin would instead go to Washington, D.C., and ask for aid from the U.S. government.

Juan Seguín (1806–1890)

Juan Seguín was born in San Antonio in 1806. His father was active in government there and was a friend of Stephen F. Austin's. After the fighting in Goliad, Austin made Juan Seguín a captain. Seguín's men helped gather information and supplies for the Texians. They also took part in the fighting in San Antonio in December 1835. After the Texian defeat at the Alamo, Seguín fought at San Jacinto. He then served in the new Texas government. During the 1840s, he was forced to flee Texas. Tensions between Texians and Tejanos had grown since the revolution. The Texians wanted to control more of the land and the government. Seguín later returned to Texas for a time, but he spent his last years in Mexico. A town in Texas is named for him.

Bowie and His Knife

James Bowie came to Texas in the late 1820s and a few years later married a Tejana woman. Before that, he had made a fortune raising sugarcane in Louisiana. He had also won fame for his skill fighting with a knife. Bowie's brother had designed a special knife just for him. Bowie wore the knife on his belt and killed at least one person with it. Many people wanted their own "Bowie knife" and took courses on how to fight with one. Knives based on Bowie's usually had blades that were from 8 to 12 inches (20 to 30 centimeters) long. Today, hunting knives like these are still called Bowie knives.

Austin was still at San Antonio when the delegates met. His troops were camped outside the town. He wanted to attack the Mexicans, but most of his men did not. General Cos had brought cannons and placed them in the town and at the Alamo. He also had an army of about 1,400 men—about twice the size of the Texian forces.

The Texians decided not to attack, but they began a **siege**. They tried to prevent the Mexicans from getting food and more troops. Still, some goods and men did reach San Antonio. More Texians also arrived to fight, while others left.

The Grass Fight

During November, the two sides sometimes fired at each other without much effect. Finally, on November 26, they fought the first major battle of the siege. The Texians saw Mexicans leading mules toward San Antonio. A rumor spread that the mules were carrying silver for the troops. Bowie led a force of about 40 cavalrymen against the Mexicans. Both sides sent **reinforcements** during the battle. The Texians forced the Mexicans to flee and leave behind many of the mules. Bowie and his men soon learned

Cannons like this one were used by the Texians in the fighting in San Antonio. This cannon is still at the Alamo.

that the mules were not carrying silver. Instead, they had hay for the Mexicans' horses. This battle was later called the Grass Fight.

Texian Victory

A few days later, General Cos released several prisoners from San Antonio. They told the Texian troops that the Mexicans were running low on food and supplies. The Texians might be able to

In Their Own Words

A View of the Battle

Creed Taylor was one of the Texians who took part in the attack on San Antonio and later wrote about what he saw. Here is part of what he wrote:

"With the first boom of [the] cannon, the glad words 'Forward, boys! We're going into town' rang out, and the men were in motion…. The enemy's fire increased as we drew nearer the **plaza**, where the buildings were stronger and more compact, all of them being of stone or **adobe** with flat roofs, and a wall projecting around and about four feet above the surface of the roof. These walls were manned by Mexican troops who kept up a brisk fire upon us during the day, and if they had been trained marksmen…few of us would have escaped death…. As night came the terrible [firing] of small guns and the deafening roar of the **artillery** ceased. My division had not lost a man, while the enemy had suffered heavily."

defeat them if they attacked. Some Texians were still not ready to attack. They talked about retreating. Then Ben Milam stepped up. He asked the men to join him in attacking the Mexicans. About 300 men agreed to fight.

The battle began on December 5. The Texians fired their cannons at the Alamo while Milam and the others went into the town. The Mexicans sent troops to the fort, thinking it might be attacked. That move made it easier for the Texians to enter San Antonio. Soon, though, the defenders in the town began firing on the Texians. The fighting went on from house to house and dragged on for several days. At one point, the Mexicans attacked the Texian camp outside the town, but the Texians fought them off. Finally, on December 9, General Cos agreed to surrender. The Texians had taken San Antonio. About 150 Mexicans died during the fighting. The Texians had only about 35 casualties. One of the Texians killed was Ben Milam.

After the victory, many of the Texians returned home. Others left to go attack a Mexican city. Colonel James Neill was the commander of the men who remained. As more troops left, he moved his forces out of the town and into the Alamo. He had about 80 men.

A Slave at the Alamo

Williams Travis arrived at the Alamo with his slave, Joe. Joe was not the only African American there during the later battle, but he is one of the best known. Joe was about 23 years old in 1836. During the Battle of the Alamo, he fought for the Texians. He survived the attack but was wounded by the Mexicans afterward. Joe later reported to Texas officials on the details of the battle. He was then sent back to the Travis farm. Joe escaped from there in 1837, and he remained free for the rest of his life.

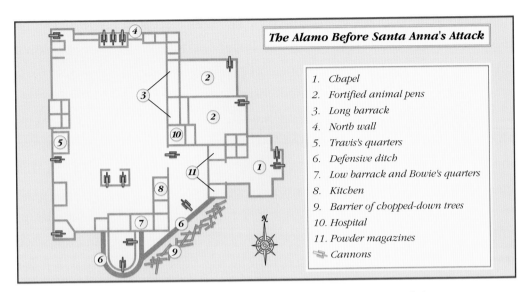

The Alamo Before Santa Anna's Attack

1. Chapel
2. Fortified animal pens
3. Long barrack
4. North wall
5. Travis's quarters
6. Defensive ditch
7. Low barrack and Bowie's quarters
8. Kitchen
9. Barrier of chopped-down trees
10. Hospital
11. Powder magazines
   Cannons

After taking over the Alamo, the Texians built fences and barriers, and they set up cannons to make the fort stronger. This map shows how the Alamo was prepared for battle in early 1836.

Preparing for Another Fight

Neill wrote a letter to Sam Houston, who was in Goliad and hoped to attack Mexico. Neill said that he had found out that a large Mexican force was on its way to San Antonio. He could not defend the town without more men and supplies. Neill also sent a similar message to Henry Smith, the governor of Texas.

Houston suggested to Smith that the Texians take their cannons out of the Alamo. They could use the guns at Goliad and another town. Then, the Alamo should be blown up. Houston sent Bowie to the Alamo to carry out this plan. But the Alamo was not blown up. Instead, Governor Smith decided that the fort was worth keeping and defending. He sent William Travis to the fort with more men.

The Texians began to prepare the fort for any Mexican attack. They put up wooden fences to close gaps in the walls. In other places, they filled in holes in the walls with dirt. The men also built platforms along the walls. From these platforms, the Texians would be able to fire down on attackers.

As this went on, Bowie learned about the Mexicans' activities. Friends of his in Texas sometimes rode to the Alamo with news. They told him about thousands of enemy troops heading toward Texas. Bowie wrote to the governor, asking for more help. Bowie also had another concern. His health was poor, and the fort doctor did not know what was wrong.

A small group of volunteers reached the Alamo on February 8, 1836. They had come from Tennessee with Davy Crockett. He and Houston were friends. Crockett had not planned to join the fight when he first left for Texas. Now, he hoped to play a role in the Texas government after its war against Mexico.

Davy Crockett (1786–1836)

Born in Tennessee in 1786, Davy Crockett was already famous when he reached the Alamo. Crockett was a soldier and bear hunter who often lived simply in the woods. He was well-liked because of his bravery and the stories he told about himself and others. Some of his tales were not true, but people enjoyed them for their humor. Crockett entered politics in 1821, and he was later elected to Congress. Some people hoped he might run for president of the United States. Several authors wrote books about his life that sold well. Fighting at the Alamo made Crockett a hero to many Americans.

Some of the Texians at the Alamo lived in this building, which can still be seen today.

On February 10 the Texians held a dance to honor Crockett. Women from the town joined the party. Late that night, word reached the Alamo that Santa Anna was heading toward San Antonio. The message said he had 13,000 troops.

This was many more troops than Santa Anna actually had. Still, Bowie and Travis knew that a large Mexican army was near. They did not end the party. But they knew that the next day they would have to start making more plans for defending the Alamo.

Chapter 4

The Battle of the Alamo

By mid-February 1836, James Bowie and William Travis shared the command of the Alamo. They continued to prepare the men for battle. They moved more cannons into place. The fort did not have many cannonballs. One soldier cut up horseshoes to fire out of the big guns. The two commanders also received news about Santa Anna. Several Tejanos rode to the fort and said the Mexicans were drawing closer.

On the morning of February 23, news spread through San Antonio. Santa Anna was now just outside the town. Some residents began to leave. Others went to the Alamo for safety. The Mexican soldiers quickly took control of the town. Travis sent a message to Gonzales asking for reinforcements. Later another request went to Goliad.

In the town, the Mexicans flew a red flag from the church tower. The flag meant Santa Anna would kill all the defenders if they did not surrender. Travis had the men fire a shot

This painting shows William Travis (at left, holding sword) encouraging his men as they prepare for Santa Anna's attack on the Alamo.

from their largest cannon. But Bowie wanted to speak with Santa Anna. He sent a message to the Mexican general. Santa Anna replied that the Texians had to surrender. Instead, Travis and Bowie decided to stay in the Alamo. They hoped enough reinforcements would come to save the fort.

Waiting for Reinforcements

Bowie was now very ill. He gave Travis full command of the Alamo. Travis sent out men to get food. The Texians had not gathered many supplies

Two Leaders at the Alamo

Colonel Neill left the Alamo in mid-February. William Travis should have taken command of the fort. He was part of the Texas army. But many of the men at the fort were volunteers. They wanted James Bowie to lead them. American **militia** had often chosen their commanders. Travis let the volunteers at the Alamo vote for their commander. They chose Bowie. He and Travis then agreed to share the command. Bowie led the volunteers and Travis led the regular soldiers.

before Santa Anna arrived. By now, about 1,500 Mexican troops were outside the Alamo. More were on their way. On February 24, Travis sent another message to Gonzales seeking reinforcements.

Santa Anna decided to wait for his own reinforcements before attacking. He set up his cannons and sometimes fired on the Alamo.

Travis eagerly waited for reinforcements too. Finally, on March 1, 32 men arrived from Gonzales. Travis hoped an even larger force would arrive from Goliad. It never came. James Fannin was the Goliad commander. He started to lead reinforcements to the Alamo. But the Goliad troops had many problems on the way. Wagons broke down, and the men ran low on supplies. They decided to turn back. On March 3, Travis learned that the Goliad troops were not coming. He knew his men had no chance to win. On March 4, another small group of volunteers reached the Alamo. The fort now had about 200 defenders. Outside, a total of 2,400 Mexican soldiers waited. On March 5, Santa Anna told most of these men they would attack the Alamo early the next morning.

The Mexican Army Attacks

On March 6, the Mexicans approached the Alamo without being noticed. They charged the fort as bugles played and men yelled. The Alamo's guards fired at the attackers. The sounds of battle woke the defenders who were still asleep. The Texians then rushed to their cannons and quickly grabbed their guns.

Shots from the cannons killed and wounded many Mexicans. But Santa Anna's troops kept coming. A few managed to climb the fort's walls and get inside. They then opened the gates, so more Mexican soldiers could stream inside.

Travis was one of the first Texians killed. He took a shot in the middle of his head. James Bowie died while still in his bed. The Mexicans swarmed over the fort's cannons. They began firing the artillery against the Texians. One shot broke down the door of the fort's **chapel**. The Mexicans rushed in and killed the defenders inside. Other defenders went from one room to another inside the fort. They kept firing as they retreated. Slowly, the Mexicans found them and killed them. A few Texians tried to surrender. The Mexicans killed them anyway.

In Their Own Words

A Plea for Help

Here is part of Williams Travis's letter of February 24, 1836, asking for reinforcements to help him defend the Alamo:

"The enemy has demanded a surrender.... Otherwise [we] are to be put to the sword if the fort is taken. I have answered the demand with a cannon shot, and our flag still waves proudly from the walls. I shall never surrender nor retreat. Then, I call on you in the name of Liberty, of patriotism, and of everything dear to the American character, to come to our aid with all [speed].... If this call is [ignored], I am determined to sustain myself as long as possible and die like a soldier who never forgets what is due to his own honor and that of his country. Victory or Death."

Alamo Survivor

One of the Alamo survivors was Susanna Dickinson. Her husband had volunteered to fight the Mexicans. She and her daughter arrived in San Antonio in December 1835 and moved into the Alamo the next February. Dickinson was the only white American woman in the fort. The other women were either Tejanas or African Americans. After the battle, Dickinson met General Santa Anna. He gave her a blanket and some silver before releasing her. Later she gave Texas officials details of the fight. She described how the Mexicans fired at the fort before the March 6 attack. None of these shots killed any of the defenders. She also noted seeing Davy Crockett dead after the battle.

In this painting, Texian defenders fight to the death during the Battle of the Alamo.

Mexican soldiers tracked down Texians who managed to flee the Alamo. The soldiers killed them too. In all, about 182 Texians died. Only a few survived the attack. Most of the survivors were women and children who had sought safety in the fort. The Texians managed to kill or wound more than 300 Mexicans.

Texas Independence

By this time, the Texians had declared their independence. Sam Houston was trying to create an army that would be able to defeat Santa Anna. He told Fannin to pull his troops out of Goliad. Fannin, though, failed to act in time. Some of Santa Anna's troops advanced on Goliad. Fannin began his retreat when they were close by. The Mexicans defeated the Texians from Goliad on March 20. Santa Anna ordered that hundreds of Texian prisoners be killed. This brutal act angered the Texians still fighting for independence.

Sam Houston (right) led the Texian army that defeated Santa Anna in the final battle of the Texas Revolution.

Lone Star Flag

After winning its independence, Texas was sometimes called the Lone Star Republic. Its flag had a single white star on a blue bar. To the right of the bar were white and red stripes. Today Texas still uses the same flag and is called the Lone Star State. Texans are proud that their state was once an independent country. Only Hawaii can make the same claim.

By April, Santa Anna was chasing Houston's forces. For a time Houston set up a camp to train his men near the Colorado River. Then, he began to move again. Scouts told him where the Mexican forces were. Finally, on April 19, Houston made plans to fight Santa Anna. The two armies were near the San Jacinto River in eastern Texas. The next day, a few cavalry from each side fought a small battle near some woods. Houston kept most of his men in the trees to protect them.

Overnight, more Mexican troops arrived. Santa Anna now had about 1,200 men. Houston had about 700. Houston decided not to wait for the Mexicans to attack. On April 21, the Texians surprised Santa Anna and his men by attacking first. The men ran into battle yelling. "Remember the Alamo! Remember Goliad!" The Texians needed just 18 minutes to kill hundreds of Mexican soldiers and win the battle.

Santa Anna fled San Jacinto on horseback. The Texians found him and captured him the next day. The Mexican general then sent word to his troops that had not reached San Jacinto. He told these troops that they should return to Mexico.

A few weeks later, Santa Anna signed two treaties with the Texians. One said the fighting would end in Texas. The other said Santa Anna would grant Texas its independence. Santa Anna, however, had lost control in Mexico. The new leaders did not accept that Texas was independent.

After the Battle of San Jacinto, the Texians captured Santa Anna (in this painting he is standing and wearing white pants and a short blue jacket). Sam Houston, wounded and lying on the ground, talks with Santa Anna.

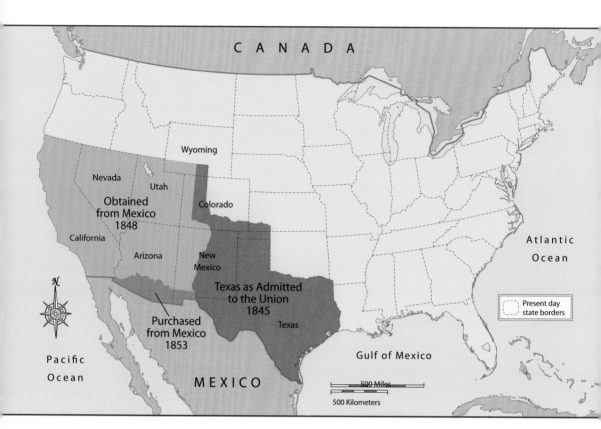

The United States added huge amounts of land that had been part of Mexico after it admitted Texas, won the Mexican-American War in 1848, and bought a strip of land from Mexico in 1853.

Still, the Texians believed they were now independent. They elected Sam Houston the first president of the Republic of Texas. Many Mexicans were angry with the Texians for rebelling and winning their freedom. They were also angry with the United States. Some Mexicans blamed it for the Texas rebellion, since most Texians had come from the United States.

Part of the United States

Mexico wanted Texas back, and in 1842 its troops invaded. The soldiers reached San Antonio, but the Texians drove them out. Even before this, some Texians wanted Texas to join the United States. Being a U.S. state would better protect them from Mexico. For a time, some U.S. leaders in Congress blocked the admission of Texas to the **Union**. Texas allowed slavery, and these leaders did not want another slave state becoming part of the United States. But in 1845, Congress did admit Texas as the 28th U.S. state. The United States claimed that Texas included more land than Mexico thought it did.

President James K. Polk welcomed Texas into the Union. He wanted to gain as much new land in the west as possible for the United States. Letting Texas join the Union angered the Mexican government even more. But it did not want to go to war over Texas. Polk, however, wanted more of Mexico's lands. He was ready to fight to get it.

The Mexican-American War

Polk sent U.S. troops from Texas south into an area that he said was part of Texas but that Mexico did not accept as part of Texas. When Mexican soldiers fought the American troops on April 25, 1846, Polk had a reason to declare war on Mexico. The Mexican-American War lasted for two years (1846–1848), and it ended with a victory for the United States. In the treaty ending the war, Mexico agreed to give up any claims to Texas, which was now firmly part of the United States. Mexico also gave up to the United States a huge amount of land in the Southwest. This area included what are now the states of California, Nevada, and Utah, most of Arizona, and parts of New Mexico, Colorado, and Wyoming.

A few years later, in 1853, the United States bought from Mexico some more land in what is now Arizona and New Mexico. The United States wanted this land in order to build a new railroad to southern California.

The events that started with Texas's battle for independence in 1836 ended less than twenty years later with the United States becoming a much larger and more powerful country.

Visiting the Alamo Today

After the Battle of the Alamo, Mexican troops remained at the fort until May 1836. Before they left, they knocked down part of the walls. Today, only two parts of the original Alamo still stand. These are one section of a building called the Long **Barrack** and the Alamo Chapel. Both buildings have been rebuilt over the years.

For a time, the U.S Army kept supplies at the Alamo. A store also opened on the site. In 1883, the state of Texas bought the Chapel. In 1905, the state gave control of the Chapel and the Long Barrack to the Daughters of the Republic of Texas. The state wanted them to take care of the Alamo and honor the men who died there in 1836.

Visiting the Shrine

Each year, about 2.5 million people visit the Alamo. The site covers just over 4 acres (1.6 hectares). Every half-hour, tour guides give a

Millions of people from all over visit the Alamo each year. This picture shows a special ceremony held by the Daughters of the Republic of Texas to honor heroes of the Texas Revolution.

Helpful Daughters

In 1891, a group of women formed the Daughters of the Republic of Texas (DRT). They all had relatives who had lived in Texas before it became a U.S. state in 1845. The women wanted to honor the Texians who had won independence from Mexico. The women also wanted to study the history of the Texas Revolution and the Lone Star Republic. The DRT began working to save historic buildings. One of the first was the Long Barrack at the Alamo. Today, the DRT runs several other historic sites in Texas. These include a library at the Alamo. The DRT also places markers across the state noting where important events took place.

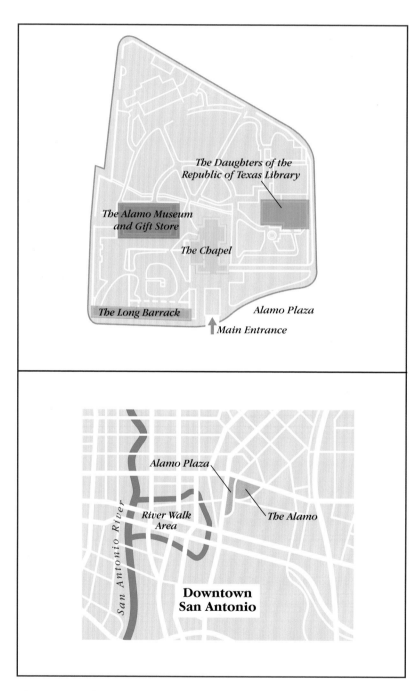

These maps show the grounds of the Alamo today and the location of the Alamo in the center of San Antonio.

The Long Barrack (above) is now a museum where visitors can learn about the history of the Alamo.

brief talk on the history the Alamo. Guests can also take an **audio** tour. Listening through headphones, they hear extra information at different spots on the site. The audio tour also includes music and the sounds of battle.

Most people begin their visit at the Chapel. Today it is called the Shrine. Men must remove their hats to honor the Texans who died in and around the building. For the same reasons, visitors are asked to speak quietly

A Line in the Sand?

For years, many people talked about the "line in the sand" at the Alamo. William Travis was said to have gathered his men on March 5. He told them that they would most likely die when the Mexican army attacked. Still, he would stay and defend the Alamo. Then he drew a line in the sand with his sword. He said the men who would stay with him and fight should cross over the line. All but one did. Today a marker at the Alamo tells the story of the line in the sand. But most historians now doubt that Travis drew one. The tale about the line was created many years later to show the bravery of the Alamo defenders.

inside. The Shrine has items that belonged to some of the defenders. You can see a rifle that was used during the battle and a ring William Travis once wore. There is also a deerskin vest that Davy Crockett wore. The Chapel has flags of different states and countries. These flags show places from which the defenders came before reaching Texas. A large number came from Tennessee, Kentucky, and Virginia. About 30 had been born in Ireland and Great Britain. Two came from Germany.

Like the Chapel, the Long Barrack also serves as a museum. An exhibit explains the history of the Alamo from its beginning as a Spanish mission. The building also has a small movie theater. You can watch a film on the history of the Alamo.

The third building at the site is the Museum and Gift Store. It was built in 1936. Here you can learn more about the Alamo's past and Texas history. Some special exhibits have featured items the Mexican troops used during the Texas Revolution. Others have looked at the weapons both sides used. These include the Bowie knife. In the center of the museum is a model showing the Alamo during the battle. Tiny figures of Mexican and

This monument in Alamo Plaza shows some of the defenders of the Alamo and honors all of the people who died there.

Texian troops surround the fort. The museum also has a shop that sells books and items related to Texas history.

Outside the buildings is the Wall of History. This exhibit has more information on the Alamo. The grounds also include beautiful gardens and a large oak tree. You can also see a few cannons that were used during the battle. Some **plaques** outside mark important events. One shows a copy of the first letter William Travis wrote seeking help for the Alamo.

Alamo Plaza

Outside the main buildings is Alamo Plaza. Parts of the original mission stood here. A plaque shows where the Low Barrack stood. James Bowie spent time there during his illness. Stones in the plaza show the spot where Davy Crockett helped defend the fort. Another marker shows where the Mexicans burned the bodies of the dead Texians.

The plaza also has a stone monument called the Cenotaph. (A cenotaph is a monument that is put up to honor a person or group of people who are not buried at the place where it stands.) It honors the men who died at the Alamo. The monument stands 60 feet (18 meters) tall. At the bottom are statues of some of the defenders. The most famous ones shown are Crockett, Travis, and Bowie.

Honoring Bravery

At the Alamo, visitors see and learn about an important part of history. Steve Hardin is a historian of the Alamo. He has said this about visiting this shrine: "You cannot help but be aware that, on this very spot, brave men fought and died for a cause they believed to be larger than themselves." That cause was freedom. Americans will always remember the bravery of the Alamo defenders. They will always value the courage people show in defense of freedom.

The City of San Antonio

Since 1836, the town of San Antonio has become a city. It now surrounds the Alamo and its grounds. The city has a population of about 1.3 million people, making it one of the largest in the United States. The Alamo is close to another popular San Antonio spot called the River Walk (below). A stone pathway follows a branch of the San Antonio River. Shops, hotels, restaurants, and museums line the walk. Street musicians often play on it. And visitors can take boat trips from one end to the other. San Antonio is also known for four other missions built around the time of the Alamo. The city also has the 750-foot- (230-meter-) tall Tower of the Americas. At the top is a restaurant that slowly turns.

Timeline ★ ★ ★ ★ ★ ★ ★ ★

★ **1718**   Work begins on the first Mission San Antonio de Valero.

★ **1724**   The mission moves to its final location, the site of today's Alamo.

★ **1793**   The mission closes.

★ **1803**   Spanish soldiers turn the mission into a fort.

★ **1810–1821**   Mexico fights for and wins its independence from Spain.

★ **1821**   Stephen F. Austin begins to bring settlers from the United States into Texas, which is part of Mexico.

★ **1824**   Texas becomes part of the Mexican state of Coahuila y Texas.

★ **1830**   Mexico angers Texians when it limits American immigration to Texas.

★ **1835**   **October:** The Texas Revolution begins in Gonzales as Texians stop Mexican troops from taking a cannon kept there.
December: Texians drive Mexican forces out of San Antonio and station troops in the Alamo.

★ **1836**   **February:** Several thousand Mexican troops reach San Antonio to take back the Alamo.
March: The Texians declare their independence from Mexico. Mexican forces under General Santa Anna defeat the Texians at the Battle of the Alamo.
April: The Texians win the Battle of San Jacinto, giving them their independence.

★ **1845**   Texas joins the United States, becoming the 28th state.

★ **1846–1848**   The United States defeats Mexico in the Mexican-American War. As a result, Mexico gives up all claims to Texas and gives the United States a large amount of land in the Southwest.

★ **1883**   The state of Texas buys the Alamo Chapel.

★ **1903**   The Daughters of the Republic of Texas (DRT) buy the other remaining building at the Alamo.

★ **1905**   The DRT opens the Alamo as a shrine.

adobe: bricks made of clay dried in the sun.

Anglo: a white American who is not of Spanish or Mexican descent.

artillery: cannons and other large guns that fire cannonballs, shells filled with explosives, or other objects over long distances.

audio: relating to sound or hearing.

barrack: a building where groups of people sleep.

casualties: soldiers killed, wounded, missing, or taken prisoner during a battle.

cavalry: soldiers who fight on horseback.

chapel: a small building or part of a building used for religious services.

colony: an area that is owned and controlled by another country and is not independent.

constitution: a document that outlines a country's or a state's form of government and how laws are made and enforced.

delegates: people chosen to represent others at a meeting.

dictator: a leader who rules with complete power.

exile: having to live outside one's own country.

immigrant: a person who leaves one country to settle in another.

militia: citizens who train as soldiers and fight when needed.

mission: a small settlement built around a Roman Catholic church; the settlement had other buildings and land around the church, and priests who lived at the mission tried to teach their religion to the local people.

plaques: flat, thin pieces of metal or wood with writing on them.

plaza: an open area in the center of a town surrounded by buildings.

rebels: people who try to change their government by using force.

rebellion: violence used to overthrow leaders or a government.

reinforcements: extra soldiers sent into a battle.

republic: a form of government in which voters choose people to make laws and run the government for them.

shrine: a place considered special because of past events there.

siege: an effort to defeat an enemy army in a fort or other place by surrounding the place and preventing the army from receiving supplies or more troops.

treason: actions taken to harm one's country.

Union: another name for the United States.

To Learn More ★ ★ ★ ★ ★ ★

Read these books

Bankston, John. *Antonio López de Santa Anna*. Bear, Del.: Mitchell Lane, 2004.

Collard, Sneed B. *David Crockett: Fearless Frontiersman*. New York: Marshall Cavendish, 2007.

Edmondson, J. R. *Jim Bowie: Frontier Legend, Alamo Hero*. New York: PowerPlus Books, 2003.

Gunderson, Cory Gideon. *The Battle of the Alamo*. Edina, Minn.: Abdo Daughters, 2004.

Schaefer, Ted, and Lola Schaefer. *The Alamo*. Chicago: Heinemann Library, 2006.

Steele, Christy. *Texas Joins the United States*. Milwaukee: World Almanac Library, 2005.

Walker, Paul Robert. *Remember the Alamo: Texians, Tejanos, and Mexicans Tell Their Stories*. Washington, D.C.: National Geographic, 2007.

Look up these Web sites

The Alamo official Web site
http://www.thealamo.org/main.html

Explorations—Remembering the Alamo
http://www.digitalhistory.uh.edu/learning_history/alamo/alamo_preparations.cfm

The Battle of the Alamo
http://www.tsl.state.tx.us/treasures/republic/alamo-01.html

The Handbook of Texas Online
http://www.tshaonline.org

Remember the Alamo
http://www.pbs.org/wgbh/amex/alamo/index.html

In the Alamo's Shadow
http://www.tamu.edu/ccbn/dewitt/adp/history/1836/blacks/jackson.html

The Second Flying Company of Alamo de Parras
http://www.tamu.edu/ccbn/dewitt/adp/toc.html

Key Internet search terms

Alamo, Stephen F. Austin, James Bowie, Davy Crockett, Sam Houston, San Antonio, Texas history, William Travis

The abbreviation *ill.* stands for illustration, and *ills.* stands for illustrations. Page references to illustrations and maps are in *italic* type.

Index ★ ★ ★ ★ ★ ★ ★ ★ ★

★ ★

About the Author

Michael Burgan is a former editor at *Weekly Reader,* where he wrote about current events. As a freelance author, he has written more than 150 books for children and young adults, mostly nonfiction. His specialties are U.S. history and biographies of world figures. He is also a playwright. Burgan has a B.A. in history from the University of Connecticut and currently lives with his wife in Chicago.